Bible Stories for Children
The
New Testament

Bible Stories for Children
The
New Testament

Retold by Vic Parker

Miles
KeLLy

First published in 2011 by Miles Kelly Publishing Ltd
Harding's Barn, Bardfield End Green, Thaxted, Essex, CM6 3PX, UK

2 4 6 8 10 9 7 5 3 1

Editorial Director Belinda Gallagher
Art Director Jo Cowan
Editor Carly Blake
Designers Michelle Foster, Joe Jones
Cover/Junior Designer Kayleigh Allen
Consultant Janet Dyson
Production Manager Elizabeth Collins
Reprographics Stephan Davis, Ian Paulyn

ISBN 978-1-84810-406-8

Printed in China

British Library Cataloguing-in-Publication Data
A catalogue record for this book is available from the British Library

ACKNOWLEDGEMENTS
The publishers would like to thank the following artists
who have contributed to this book:

The Bright Agency Katriona Chapman, Dan Crisp,
Giuliano Ferri (inc. cover), Mélanie Florian

Advocate Art Andy Catling, Alida Massari

*The publishers would like to thank Robert Willoughby and
the London School of Theology for their help in compiling this book.*

Made with paper from a sustainable forest

www.mileskelly.net   info@mileskelly.net

www.factsforprojects.com

Self-publish your
children's book

buddingpress.co.uk

Contents

Introduction

THE NEW TESTAMENT is the name for the second section of the Bible, made up of twenty-seven books. It describes the birth, life and death of a man called Jesus, His teachings about God and His followers.

Jesus lived two thousand years ago in the Middle East. At that time, the Romans controlled these lands and the Jewish people who lived there were unhappy about it. They were waiting for a saviour —

the 'Messiah' – who would establish a
mighty kingdom for them. The New
Testament was written by the followers
of Jesus, who believed Him to be the Messiah,
during the one hundred years after He died.

At the beginning of each story is
a short introduction. This helps
to set the scene by providing
information about the time
period, events and characters.

The Birth of Jesus

*When Jesus was born, the Romans ruled over the land.
The Roman Emperor wanted to make a count of all the people,
so Mary and Joseph had to travel to Joseph's home town of Bethlehem.
This is the town where Ruth and Boaz had lived and the birthplace
of their great-grandson, King David.*

In the town of Nazareth lived a woman called Mary, who was engaged to marry a young man called Joseph, a local carpenter. When she told Joseph she was expecting a baby he was very upset. The baby couldn't be his because they weren't married. And in those days, if a single

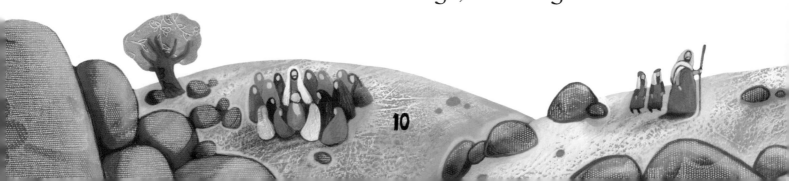

woman was expecting a baby it was quite shameful. However, Joseph had a dream in which an angel told him, "Don't be afraid to take Mary as your wife. Her baby is the Son of God Himself. The prophets of long ago foretold that He would come and save everyone from their sins. Raise Him as your own son. God wants you to call Him Jesus." After this Joseph felt much better. He realized he would be honoured to bring the little boy up as his own, and he and Mary married straight away.

However, near the time that the baby was to be born, another problem arose. The emperor Augustus Caesar ordered a survey of all the people in his lands. He commanded that every man had to travel

to where he was born, taking his family with him to have their names put on a register. Joseph had been born in the city of Bethlehem in Judea, in southern Israel, which was quite a distance from the village of Nazareth. Mary was heavily pregnant and travelling would be very difficult for her. Nevertheless, the couple did not have a choice. They packed what they would need for the trip and set off. Mary couldn't possibly walk all that way, so she rode on a donkey. It was a bumpy and tiring journey for a woman so close to having a baby.

By the time the couple reached Bethlehem they were exhausted, hungry and dusty. Joseph began trying to find a room in which they could stay. He trudged with the donkey and Mary from one lodging place to the next. But to the couple's dismay, everywhere was full. The city was bustling with travellers who had come to register for the emperor's survey.

As they were turned away from one place after another, Mary began to feel that the baby was on its way. Hurriedly, Joseph banged on the door of the nearest inn. After a few moments, the busy innkeeper peered outside. "Don't bother asking, we're full," he said, as soon as he saw the travellers.

"Wait, please help us!" cried Joseph,

stopping the innkeeper from shutting the door on them. "My wife's about to have a baby. She can't give birth out here in the street! Haven't you got a spare corner somewhere you could squeeze us in?"

"Well…" said the innkeeper, looking at poor Mary in pain on the donkey. "I haven't got a single room to spare, but you're welcome to shelter in my stable if you don't mind the animals."

"Thank you, thank you so much," Joseph said, gratefully shaking the man's hand, and the innkeeper showed them the way to his stable.

It was there, with the donkeys, oxen and sheep looking on, that Mary gave birth to the baby boy who was to be the saviour of

the world. She wrapped Him up in cloths
and nestled Him in a manger full of straw.
And baby Jesus was warm and safe, with
His mother and foster father by His side.

Matthew chapter 1; Luke chapter 2

The Shepherds' Visit

*Jesus was born in a simple stable, surrounded by
sheep and oxen. The first visitors to the newborn baby
were hard-working shepherds who recognized that
Jesus was a very special child.*

On the night that Jesus was born, the
city of Bethlehem throbbed with
people, while the surrounding countryside
was peaceful except for a few shepherds and
their flocks. The shepherds were taking turns
at sleeping and watching. They made sure
that the sheep weren't wandering away and

kept watch for hungry wolves.

All at once the starry night sky above the shepherds blazed as bright as day. Then it blazed brighter still, too bright for the shepherds to look up. They shielded their eyes from the blinding glare as an angel appeared high overhead. The shepherds were terrified.

"Don't be afraid," came the angel's voice, clear through the still, cold night. "I bring you wonderful news – wonderful news for everyone on Earth. This very night a child has been born who will be the saviour of all people. You can find Him in a stable in Bethlehem, lying in a manger."

The air was filled with singing more beautiful than the shepherds had ever heard,

as hundreds of thousands of angels suddenly appeared in the heavens. "Glory to God," they sang. "And peace to all people on Earth."

The shepherds stood transfixed until the angels had finished their song. Then the heavenly music died and the angels faded away.

Could it really be true the shepherds wondered? In ancient stories prophets had predicted for hundreds of years that a man would come who would save everyone from their sins. They called him the Messiah. Maybe he had really come at last. The shepherds hurried off to Bethlehem,

to see for themselves. They searched through the streets until they heard the sound of a newborn baby crying from a stable behind an inn. There they found Mary and Joseph looking after baby Jesus. In great excitement, they told the startled couple all that they had seen and heard. Mary fell very quiet, taking it all in.

The shepherds stayed for a while, marvelling at the baby boy who they had been told was the Messiah, but they had to return to their flocks. All the way back they couldn't stop talking about the amazing chorus of angels and how their

words had come true. They told everyone
they met, praising God and giving thanks
for all that they had seen and been told.

Luke chapter 2

Follow the Star

*The wise men travelled many miles to see baby Jesus,
following a bright star in the sky. They brought with them
exotic gifts, fit for a king. Like the shepherds, they somehow
knew that Jesus was special.*

Far away in distant lands to the east,
there lived some wise men who were
astrologers. Every night they gazed up at
the sky and studied the stars, trying to work
out what their movements around the
heavens meant for people on Earth. One
night they were stunned by a brand new

star that appeared much bigger and brighter than the rest. They hurried to consult their ancient books to see what it could mean. The wise men became very excited by what they found, and were in no doubt that a great Jewish prophecy had come true. The star was a sign that a baby had been born who would become the king of God's Chosen People. The wise men decided to set off to find him at once. They loaded up their camels with supplies and set off into the desert, heading in the direction of the star that blazed each night in the sky. Finally, they arrived in the city of Jerusalem.

News soon reached King Herod of Judea that strangers from the east had arrived in

Jerusalem. These strangers were searching for a newborn baby they were calling the 'King of the Jews'. Of course Herod didn't like the sound of that at all. As far as he was concerned he had been crowned King of the Jews and he wanted it to stay that way. He certainly wasn't going to put up with rumours spreading about a rival – who fulfilled one of the ancient prophecies no less. It would just stir up trouble among the people and they might rise up against him.

King Herod set about dealing with the problem in his cold, calculated way. First, he called a meeting of all the chief Jewish religious leaders to find out more. "Where do your ancient books say the Messiah is to be born?" he asked, innocently.

"In Bethlehem," the holy men answered.

Then King Herod called his guards and ordered them to find the wise men and bring them to him. "But do it in secret," he commanded. "I don't want people to get the impression that I think these men and their rumours are important."

The wise men were nervous when they were summoned to see the king. They had heard that Herod could be a cruel leader. However, they were surprised to find him most polite, interested and even helpful in their quest. "The Jewish elders have told me that you shouldn't be looking in Jerusalem," he explained. "Try Bethlehem instead. When you have found the future king, do come back and tell me all about it.

I'd like to go and pay my respects too."

The wise men had no idea that King Herod only wanted to know where the baby was so he could have him killed.

They set off to Bethlehem and followed the star to where it appeared to hang biggest and brightest in the sky, over the house in which Mary and Joseph were now staying. The wise men were surprised to find the baby in an ordinary home rather than a splendid palace. They bowed to worship Him and presented Mary and Joseph with gifts – jewelled gold caskets, and the rare spices frankincense and myrrh.

Herod never got to hear of the wise men's success. The night before they were due to set off home, they had a troubling dream that warned them not to return to the king. The wise men took a different route back to their lands in the east and Herod never found them.

Matthew chapter 2

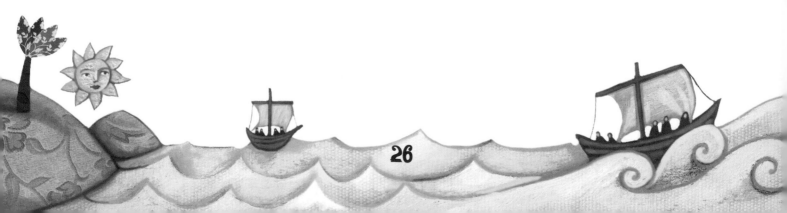

Flight from Danger

Soon after Jesus was born, Mary and Joseph were forced to leave Bethlehem. They travelled many miles south to Egypt to escape cruel King Herod.

After the wise men had visited Jesus, an angel appeared to Joseph in a dream. "Herod is trying to find the baby to kill Him," the angel warned. "Take Him and Mary to Egypt. It will be a long, hard journey, but it will take you safely out of the cruel king's reach. Stay there until I tell

you it is safe to return."

Joseph woke up with a start. He woke Mary and told her to make ready to travel straight away. The family hurried through the dark, sleeping streets of Bethlehem and onto the road to Egypt.

Meanwhile back in Jerusalem, Herod was waiting for the wise men to return from Bethlehem and tell him where the baby king of kings was. He waited… and waited… Eventually he realized that the wise men weren't coming – he had been tricked! Herod flew into a fury and roared at his army chief, "Send your men to search every house in Bethlehem.

I want every boy under two years of age put to death immediately!"

By the time the soldiers arrived in Bethlehem to carry out their terrible task, Jesus, Mary and Joseph were miles away in Egypt. They stayed there for several months until an angel appeared to Joseph once more, telling him that King Herod had died and it was safe to go back to Israel.

However Joseph did not take his family back to Bethlehem. The city was far too close to Jerusalem, where King Herod's son was now on the throne. Instead, he travelled north back to their home in the sleepy town of Nazareth in the remote area of Galilee.

Matthew chapter 2

Jesus in the Temple

During the festival of Passover, when Jesus was twelve years old, He became separated from His parents. When Mary and Joseph found Him in the temple, Jesus had begun to realize He had a special relationship with God.

Every year at the festival of Passover, all Jewish men went to visit the temple in Jerusalem to pray and give thanks to God. Joseph always went and, like many women, Mary went too. Of course the number of people who crowded into the city was huge. The lodging houses were heaving, people packed streets and the temple itself was totally crammed. Like many parents with young children, Mary and Joseph left Jesus with a relative or neighbour when they went to celebrate the festival. But when He reached the age of twelve, they decided Jesus was old enough to go with them.

The family travelled to Jerusalem with a large group of relatives and friends. When the festival was over, they all set off to travel home. Joseph walked with the men, Mary chatted to the women and Jesus ran back and forth with the other children.

But at the end of the first day's journey, when the group of travellers began to make camp for the night, Jesus had disappeared. Mary and Joseph called for their son at the tops of their voices, but He didn't come. With a rising sense of panic, the couple dashed up and down, describing Jesus to everyone and asking if anyone had seen Him. No one had. Darkness was drawing in fast. "There's nothing else we can do tonight, but as soon as it gets light tomorrow we'll retrace our steps and find Him," Joseph comforted his weeping wife.

Of course, Mary and Joseph didn't sleep for worrying about where Jesus was and whether He was safe. At sunrise Mary and Joseph began making their way back to Jerusalem, asking everyone they met if they had seen a lost twelve-year-old boy. They reached the city and hunted around its bustling streets for two days, but there was no sign of Him.

The third day came and in desperation Mary and Joseph went to look in the great temple itself. To their astonishment, there they found Jesus deep in discussion with a group of Jewish priests and leaders.

"Your son has such a wise understanding of the ancient writings, we can't believe He is only twelve," the holy men told Mary and Joseph. "He asks questions that most

people never think to ask, and He's been giving us answers too!"

But Mary and Joseph just wanted to know what had happened to Jesus. "Where on earth have you been?" They cried. "We've been worried sick!"

Jesus replied calmly, "You should have known that you would find me in my Father's house."

Luke chapter 2

John the Baptist

John was Jesus' cousin. When John baptized Jesus in the River Jordan, he recognized that Jesus was the Messiah, the long-awaited leader who would save all people. The dove in this story represents the Holy Spirit, a sign that God was with Jesus.

Mary's sister Elizabeth and her husband Zachariah had a son called John, who grew up to be a holy man. He went to live on his own in the countryside of Judea, so he could think about God and pray without being distracted. He wore only a simple robe woven from camel hair and survived by eating locusts and wild honey.

When he was about thirty years old, he began preaching to anyone he came across. "Be sorry for your sins and turn away from evil," was his message, "so you can enter God's Kingdom, which is nearly here!"

John was such a powerful speaker that people travelled especially to see him. People from all walks of life flocked from towns, villages and the city of Jerusalem too. From poor common people, to powerful Jewish groups such as the Pharisees and the Sadducees, as well as farmers, shop keepers, tax collectors and even Roman soldiers. They usually found John on the banks of the River Jordan.

"What does God want from us?" they

would ask.

John would advise, "Be kind and generous. Treat each other fairly. Don't hurt anyone, neither in your actions nor words."

John's teachings were so stirring that people often asked him if he was the saviour – the Messiah spoken of in the ancient writings. "No," John would insist, "but I am trying to prepare the way for His coming."

One after the other, people would tell John all the things they had done wrong in their lives, hanging their heads in shame. They felt truly sorry for their sins and promised they wouldn't do them again, and that they would turn to God and try to live by His rules. Then John baptized them in the holy river. He dipped the people into the water and gave them God's blessing, so their sins were washed away and they could begin afresh. "I'm only baptizing you with water," John told them, "but the man who is coming will baptize you with the fire of the Holy Spirit. He is so holy that I am not even good enough to undo his sandals."

One day, among the crowd on the banks of the Jordan, Jesus was waiting to be baptized. John knew who He was immediately. "It's not right that I baptize you," John told Jesus. "You should be baptizing me."

But Jesus insisted that it was what God wanted. So together the men walked into the river. As soon as John had baptized Jesus, the clouds above them parted and light blazed down on Jesus. A dove came gliding down and hovered above Jesus, and John knew that it was God's Holy Spirit coming down to Him. Then a voice spoke into everyone's minds saying, "This is my beloved son, with whom I am very pleased."

Matthew chapter 3;
Mark chapter 1; Luke chapter 3;
John chapter 1

Jesus' First Miracle

Some people were already beginning to see that Jesus was not just an ordinary boy, but someone remarkable. In this story Jesus reveals His ability to perform miracles by turning water into wine at a wedding. This was the first sign of more amazing things to come.

Jesus left the River Jordan and the desert lands of Judea in the south behind Him and went back to live in Galilee in the north. He knew God wanted Him to begin teaching everyone what they had to do to enter His Kingdom. Several followers of John the Baptist went with Jesus to help.

Jesus preached in Jewish places of worship called synagogues. "Beg God to forgive your sins," He told everyone, just like John the Baptist had, "so you can enter the Kingdom of God, which is coming." News soon spread that Jesus was an exciting speaker and He quickly built a following.

Not long after Jesus had arrived back in Galilee, His mother Mary told Him that they had been invited to a wedding in Cana. It was to be a big event and the wedding celebrations were set to go on for several days.

Sitting down at the feast for the wedding, everyone was having a wonderful time. About halfway through, Mary noticed that the wine was starting to run out. She knew

it would be highly embarrassing for the bride and bridegroom if they couldn't offer their guests any more to drink. So she whispered to Jesus, feeling sure that He could help.

"I'm sorry but I can't do anything about it," Jesus whispered back. "It's not a good time right now."

But Mary turned to the flustered servants and said, "I've noticed that you are low on wine, but my son can help. Do exactly what He says."

Jesus sighed. He gave his mother a gentle smile. Then He told the servants, "Fill all the empty wine jars up to the brim with water." They hurried to do as He said. "Now pour some into a goblet and take it to your boss, the steward, for tasting," Jesus instructed. They did so, rather worried, but to their astonishment the steward smacked his lips, clapped his hands and ordered it to be served to the guests at once. The water had turned into wine. Not only that, but excellent wine – better than they had previously been serving. The steward strode straight over to the bridegroom to congratulate him on his good taste and generosity.

Through the power of God His Father, Jesus had performed His first miracle. There were many more to come.

Matthew chapter 4; Mark chapter 1; Luke chapter 4; John chapters 1, 2

Jesus Goes Fishing

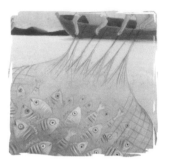

Peter was a fisherman and one of Jesus' closest friends. After he witnessed Jesus perform a miracle, Peter realized that only someone filled with God's power could do this. From that moment on, Peter and the other fishermen decided to follow Jesus and help Him.

Jesus sailed out on the Sea of Galilee in a boat belonging to two of His followers, Peter and Andrew, who were fishermen. "Throw your nets into the water. Let's see if there are any fish today," Jesus suggested.

"We already know there aren't," Peter replied gloomily. "We were fishing all last

night and we didn't catch a thing."

"Well, why not try again?" Jesus urged.

"I don't think there's much point," Peter shrugged. Then he saw a strange gleam in Jesus' eyes. "But I suppose there's no harm in having another go."

He and Andrew lowered their nets and waited… Then after a while, the brothers went to lift them up again. To their astonishment, the nets were so heavy with fish that they couldn't raise them. The stunned pair had to signal for help from a nearby boat, belonging to the two sons of a man called Zebedee. Their names were James and John and they rowed over to help.

Jesus watched the four men work hard together. It took all their strength to heave

the enormous catch aboard. Soon Peter and Andrew's little boat was full of shiny, wriggling fish, and so weighed down in the water that it was in danger of sinking.

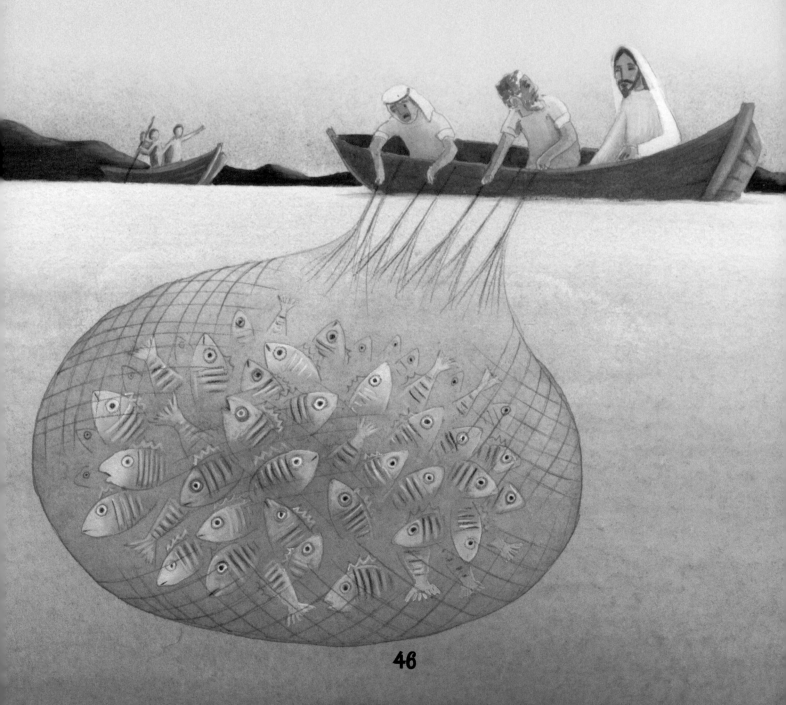

The men knew that this sort of catch was unheard of. Something miraculous must have happened. Peter fell on his knees before Jesus and said, "Lord, I'm not good enough to be one of your followers. I shouldn't have doubted what you said, I should have just done it straight away."

"Don't worry," Jesus said, kindly. "Anyway, I'm going to show you how to catch people instead of fish…"

From then on, Peter, Andrew, James and John stayed at Jesus' side and helped him.

Matthew chapter 4; Mark chapter 1; Luke chapter 5

Wonders at Capernaum

The reports of Jesus' amazing power spread across the country and people came from far and wide to see Him, listen to His teachings and to be cured of their illnesses. The people of Capernaum queued through the streets, and patiently Jesus saw every one of them.

Worshippers in synagogues who heard Jesus preach were always amazed at the way He spoke. Jesus didn't just read out the ancient holy writings as most Jewish teachers did, He actually explained them.

One day, Jesus was in the synagogue at Capernaum, in the middle of giving a speech, when a man burst out of the crowd around Him and starting shouted wildly. "I know who you are!" he yelled, pointing his finger threateningly in Jesus' face. "You're a messenger from God. And I know what you've been sent to do, you have come to destroy us all!"

As the crowd gasped in shock, Jesus remained calm. "Be quiet," He commanded. Then He shut his eyes and after a moment said sternly, "Leave him alone!"

All at once the man fainted and crumpled to the floor. When he recovered, he seemed to be a completely different person. He was quiet and calm, if somewhat confused. There had been demons inside the man, but Jesus had ordered them out.

All those who witnessed this incredible event couldn't believe their eyes and ears. Who is this Jesus of Nazareth they wondered? What sort of strange powers does He have that He is able to command demons?

Meanwhile, Jesus had gone to Peter's house. Peter told Him that his mother-in-law was very ill with an extremely high temperature and begged Jesus to visit her to see if He could help. Jesus stood by the bedside of the sick woman who was shivering and sweating with fever, and groaning in pain. Jesus took her hand and said simply but firmly, "Be well." Straight away the hot flush seemed to fade from her cheeks. She stopped writhing around and her breathing calmed. Then she opened her eyes, looked around at everyone and said, "What am I doing in bed? Peter, you should have told me we had guests. Now what would everyone like to eat and drink?" And she got up and began bustling around.

News of what happened at the synagogue and at Peter's house spread around Capernaum and the surrounding towns in no time. Before sunset, there was a long queue outside Peter's door, everyone wanting to see Jesus. People had come from miles around, begging to be cured of all sorts of illnesses.

They had brought their sick relations and friends with them too.

Very patiently, Jesus saw them all, one by one. Before the night had ended, He had placed his hands upon every single person and they had all been cured.

Jesus left Capernaum early next morning, so as not to cause a fuss. But as soon as the

grateful townspeople realized he had gone, they tracked Him down and begged Him to stay. "I'm afraid I can't," Jesus insisted. "People in other places need me. I have to tell everyone how they can find happiness by turning to God. It is what I have been sent to do." And He and His followers, called disciples, went on their way.

Matthew chapters 7, 8; Luke chapter 4

Jesus the Healer

Jesus continued to cure many people of their illnesses.
This story tells how Jesus also used His power to help people who
were regarded as outcasts, such as lepers, and people who were not
Jewish, because they had faith and trusted in Him.

Soon people from far and wide came to hear about Jesus. Men, women and children were excited by the sound of this captivating preacher who worked miracles. They began seeking Jesus out, travelling to wherever He was to see Him for themselves. Jesus tried to help as many people as He could and convince them to turn to God.

After Jesus had preached in one place, a man who was suffering from the terrible skin disease leprosy crept up to Him. He was extremely nervous about approaching Jesus. Leprosy was very contagious and also incurable, and most people didn't want lepers anywhere near them. In fact, people usually ran away when they saw a leper coming. But Jesus didn't. The poor man knelt before Him, his skin misshapen and ugly with sores, and said, "I know that you can cure me, if you want to."

"Of course I want to," Jesus murmured, and He reached out and placed His hand on the leper's crumbling skin.

It took a couple of moments for the leper

to recover from the shock. After all, most people wouldn't dream of touching him.

But then the man looked at his hands, his legs and felt his face. His skin was healed. He was cured!

"Don't tell anyone," Jesus told the man, who was sobbing his gratitude. "Just go to your priest so he can see for himself and make an offering of thanks to God."

Another time, Jesus shocked many people when He helped an officer in the Roman army. After all, most Jewish people hated the Romans because they had taken control of Israel. The Roman officer begged Jesus to help his servant who was lying ill at home in great pain. "I will come with you straight away," Jesus told the Roman officer.

"That won't be necessary," the Roman insisted. "I know if you just give the word for my servant to recover, he will do so."

Jesus was stunned and delighted. "I haven't met a Jewish person who has shown as much faith as this," He said. "There will be many people from far-off lands who will be able to enter the Kingdom of Heaven, while many from the nation of Israel will be locked outside."

The Roman officer returned home to find his servant completely cured.

Matthew chapter 8; Mark chapter 1; Luke chapter 7; John chapter 4

Jesus Forgives Sins

Many people believed they suffered illness because they or their parents had sinned, or done something wrong. Jesus told people their sins were forgiven, but this upset the Jewish religious leaders. They accused Jesus of the being disrespectful because only God could forgive sins.

One day Jesus was preaching in a house in Capernaum that was full of people. Many of them were important Jewish people such as officials, priests and Pharisees. These highly regarded elders had travelled from all over Israel to see for themselves the strange preacher everyone was talking about. They had many questions they wanted answering. Who was Jesus? Was He a trickster, or a prophet like Elijah? Was He really the Messiah spoken of in ancient holy books? And what was Jesus teaching? They didn't want Jesus leading everyone astray. After all He wasn't even a priest with training in Jewish holy laws.

There were so many people in the house. They were jammed shoulder-to-shoulder in each room and wedged into the hall, spilling out into the street. Outside there were many more, straining to hear and get a glimpse of Jesus through the windows.

While Jesus spoke, four latecomers staggered up to the house carrying a paralyzed friend on a stretcher. They were

determined to get close enough to ask Jesus to heal their companion. When they saw there was no chance of getting in the front door, they came up with a plan. They climbed up the outside stairs and onto the roof. Then they tied ropes onto the stretcher, removed some of the roof covering, and slowly and carefully lowered their friend through the gap, right in front of Jesus.

Jesus was moved by the lengths the men

had gone to. He realized they must have huge faith in Him and great love for their sick friend. He looked down at the suffering man, placed His hand on his head and said, "Take heart, your sins are forgiven."

At His words the room erupted into uproar. The Jewish officials and holy men were outraged. They could believe that Jesus might perhaps have genuine powers of healing, but no one had the power to forgive sins except God Himself. Jesus was committing a terrible sin by saying He could do so. In fact, under Jewish law it was the crime of blasphemy for which He could be severely punished.

Jesus signalled for everyone to calm down and the room gradually fell silent. He

asked, "Do you think it's easier for me to say, 'I forgive your sins,' or for me to say, 'Get up off that stretcher, you can now walk'?" The Jewish elders mumbled to each other. Of course it was easier for Jesus to say that He had done something which they couldn't see. Jesus went on, "Maybe you'll believe that God has given me the power to heal this man's soul if I heal his body too."

Jesus looked into the eyes of the man lying stiff and still on his stretcher. "My friend, get up and walk," He said.

To everyone's amazement, he did. The Jewish officials and holy men left the house with more new questions than answers.

Matthew chapter 9; Mark chapter 2; Luke chapter 5

Jesus Chooses Special Helpers

*Jesus' twelve special helpers were known as His disciples,
meaning 'learners'. (Later, they become known as apostles).
They were ordinary men – some were fishermen and one
was a tax collector. Jesus needed them to be His close friends,
and to learn how to help Him with God's work.*

Jesus became so well known that He couldn't go anywhere without being surrounded by crowds. He once climbed high up a mountain so He could be on His own. Jesus prayed to God all night. When He came down the next day, He summoned twelve men from His many disciples.

They were brothers Peter and Andrew, brothers James and John, a former follower of John the Baptist called Philip, Matthew the tax collector, a man called Simon who was a member of a Jewish group called the Zealots, a second James, and four others – Thomas, Bartholomew, Thaddaeus and Judas Iscariot.

Jesus took the twelve men to one side and spoke to them. "I want you to be my special helpers," He explained. "I want each of you to go and preach to people what I have preached. I am going to give you the power to heal the sick, just as I do. Don't accept any money for it. Don't take anything on your travels except for the clothes you are wearing, just live off people's kindness. It won't be easy – some people will ignore you, others will try to stop you spreading my message and some may even try to have you killed. But God will always be with you, looking after you, and His Holy Spirit will give you courage. And if you give up your life for me, I promise you will have a new and happier life in Heaven."

So for several weeks, the twelve men went out around the countryside, teaching and healing in Jesus' name.

Matthew chapter 10; Mark chapters 3, 6; Luke chapters 6, 9

The Sermon on the Mount

Some of the most important teachings of Jesus are found in this sermon, or speech. The prayer beginning 'Our Father' is known as the Lord's Prayer and is said by Christians all over the world more than any other.

One day a vast crowd gathered to hear Jesus speak, so He went up a hillside so that everyone could see and hear Him.

"Blessed are all those who realize that God is missing from their lives," He preached, "for they will one day enter Heaven. Blessed are all sad people, for they will be comforted. Blessed are gentle people, for all the Earth will be theirs. Blessed are those who try to live good lives, for they will be well rewarded. Blessed are those who take pity on others, for they will be shown pity too. Blessed are those with pure hearts, for they will see God. Blessed are those who work for peace, for God cares for them as His own children. Blessed are those who follow God but are made to suffer because of it – the Kingdom of Heaven will belong to them. I want you all to follow my teachings even if people make it difficult for you. I want you to be like a light, showing others the right way."

Everyone was quiet and listening so hard, you could almost hear the plants growing.

"Don't think that I am telling you to forget about the old religious teachings and rules," Jesus went on. "I'm telling you to pay more attention to them than ever. You've been told that it is a sin to kill anyone. I'm telling you that you should not even argue with anyone. You've been told that you should not take something that belongs to someone else just because you want it. I'm telling you that you shouldn't even think about it in the first place. You've been told that if someone is nasty to you, it's alright to get your own back. I'm telling you that you should forget it and do nothing.

"You should treat your enemies the same as you treat your friends. And don't hoard

68

riches and luxuries on Earth where they can be stolen or destroyed. Instead think of good deeds as coins, and try to stack them up. But don't boast – God knows everything anyway. Lastly, don't worry about everyday things such as how you are going to pay for food to eat or clothes to wear.

If you put your energy into looking for God, He will look after you in turn."

Then Jesus told everyone how to pray. "Go somewhere quiet where you can be alone," He said, "and talk to God directly, as if you were talking to a friend. Just say whatever is in your heart. If there is anything you need, ask Him for it and He will give it to you." And he taught them a special prayer beginning with the words 'Our Father'.

Jesus gave a sad smile. "If you do as I say, you will be like a wise man who builds his home on rock and it will stand firm. But if you take no notice, you will be like a fool who builds his home on sand. The wind will blow it down and the rain will wash it away, until the house is in ruins."

Matthew chapters 5 to 7; Luke chapters 6, 11

The Miracle at the Pool

Jesus always put helping people first, even if it meant disobeying religious laws. Once again He upset the Jewish religious leaders by healing a sick man on the Sabbath day, the day when no work of any kind was allowed. Trouble was brewing…

Jesus once went to Jerusalem to attend an important religious festival. While he was there, he visited a holy pool at a place called Bethesda. The pool was always surrounded by many sick and injured people. They gathered there hoping to bathe in the water and be miraculously

cured. It was believed that every so often an angel stirred up the waters and the first person to bathe in the pool when this happened would be healed. Jesus saw one man there who had been crippled for thirty-eight years. Jesus knew that he had been waiting by the pool for a very long time. Whenever the man saw ripples appear on the water, he would struggle to drag himself towards the edge of the pool. But moving was so slow and painful for him that other people always beat him to it. Even on the rare occasion that he made it to the pool first, there was no one to help him get into the water.

Jesus felt great pity for the poor man and greatly admired him for his faith and courage. He decided that the man had waited long enough for a miracle. "Stand up and pick up your mat. You can walk," Jesus said.

And to the man's astonishment and joy, he did so. He went straight to the great temple to give thanks to God, taking delight in each step he took. A group of Jewish leaders were there and recognized him. "But you were crippled!" they marvelled. "Whatever has happened to you?"

"Jesus of Nazareth cured me," the man told them, and explained everything that had happened.

Instead of being pleased, the Jewish leaders were furious. Jesus had worked yet another miracle on the holy day of rest, the Sabbath. Outraged, they grew more determined than ever to get rid of him.

John chapter 5

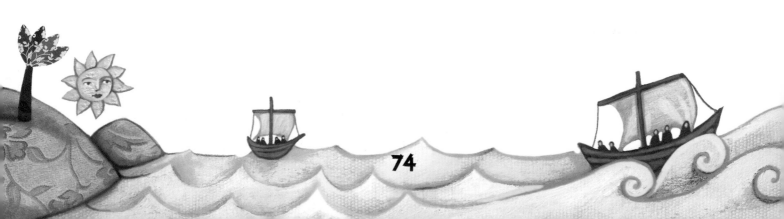

Two Fish and Five Loaves

Thousands of people had gathered to hear Jesus talk by the Sea of Galilee. Dusk fell and the crowds were still waiting for Him, so Jesus performed a miracle. He fed every single person with just a few fish and loaves that a young boy had with him.

There came a time when the King of Judea had John the Baptist, Jesus' good friend, thrown into prison and put to death. When Jesus heard the news, He was preaching at the Sea of Galilee. He was upset and wanted to escape the crowds who followed Him everywhere so He could be on His own for a little while. Jesus and His twelve disciples took a little boat out across the waters. However, the hundreds of people who had come to see and hear Jesus raced around the coast, joined by more people they met on the way. The crowd was there waiting for Jesus and His friends when they arrived on the far shore.

Jesus looked at the great mass of people – many of them sick or injured, hoping desperately for a cure. His heart went out to them. "Look at them," Jesus murmured. "They are like sheep without a shepherd."

Even though Jesus was grief-stricken and exhausted, He began preaching and healing… and was still talking to the people when dusk began to fall.

"Master, you've done enough now," the disciples said, concerned for Jesus. "It's time everyone went home. We all need something to eat."

Jesus smiled wearily. "No one needs to go anywhere," He said. "You can find us all some dinner."

The disciples looked at each other in confusion. They were surrounded by at least five thousand people. How did Jesus expect the disciples to feed them all?

"We've hardly any money between all of us to buy anything for supper," Philip pointed out.

Andrew added, "The only food we have is what this lad has brought with him," and he indicated a young boy carrying a basket.

"He's got five loaves of bread and two fish, but they'll hardly go very far!"

Jesus stretched out his hands over the loaves and fish, said a blessing and broke them into pieces. Then He told his disciples, "Now share them out among everyone."

The disciples knew that they should trust Jesus, no matter what. To their amazement, there was enough bread and fish for everybody to have a hearty supper and enough left over to fill twelve baskets.

Matthew chapter 14; Mark chapter 6; Luke chapter 9; John chapter 6

Jesus Walks on Water

In this story, Peter discovers the importance of trusting in Jesus. Peter was able to walk across the waves towards Jesus, but as soon as he doubted Him, Peter began to sink. After seeing this, the disciples realized that Jesus really was the Son of God.

It had been a long day at the Sea of Galilee. Jesus told his weary disciples to head for home without Him while He sent away the thousands of people who had gathered. "It's going to take a little while for me to convince everyone to leave," Jesus said to His friends with a sigh. "You start off without me. I want to spend some time praying on my own. I'll catch up with you soon."

"But how will you follow us?" The disciples protested, clambering into their little boats.

"Don't worry, I'll be fine," Jesus reassured, waving them off.

As the men sailed away, Jesus turned back to the crowds and told them it was time to go home too. No one wanted to leave Him, but eventually they began to wander away in groups. At last, Jesus was able to leave unnoticed and went a little way up a hillside. Finally, He had some peace and quiet and could pray alone. He stayed for quite a while, deep in thought, talking to God.

Meanwhile out on the Sea of Galilee, the disciples were in trouble. The wind had grown stronger, stirring up strong currents in the water and battering the little boats. The alarmed men rolled up the sails and tried to row to shore, but despite straining at the oars with all their might, the boats were being blown off course, and out into dangerous open waters.

Hours passed and as the night grew darker, the wind grew wilder and the waves grew higher. The disciples realized they were lost at sea and they were terrified.

As they sat huddled in their boats, desperately waiting for the light of dawn, they saw a white glow in the darkness. It

came closer and grew bigger, turning into the shape of a man.

"A ghost!" they cried, even more frightened than before. Then a voice came floating towards them on the wind.

"Don't be afraid. It's me, Jesus."

The disciples were confused. Was it really their friend and master? Or was a demon trying to trick them?

Peter spoke up bravely. "If it's really you, Lord," he shouted back, "tell me to walk to you across the waves."

"Yes, come then," Jesus called.

Peter stood up, cautiously moved to the edge of the rocking boat and took a deep breath. The other disciples could hardly believe their eyes as Peter stepped out.

Far from sinking into the churning waters, their friend strode from wave to wave, over the swirling sea, towards Jesus.

Peter kept his eyes fixed on Jesus, not daring to look down. But when he was within a couple of steps of Jesus, his curiosity got the better of him and he glanced down. The moment he saw the frothing

foam beneath his feet, his courage deserted him and he plunged down into the dark, cold waters. "Help me, Jesus!" Peter screamed in a panic. "I'm sinking!"

Jesus reached out and grabbed Peter's hand, heaving him up. "Don't doubt me," He said. "Have more faith." Jesus guided his friend back to the boats and suddenly the wind died down and the waves calmed.

The disciples had watched everything in amazement. "You really are the Son of God," they said, falling in awe at Jesus' feet.

Matthew chapter 14; Mark chapter 6; John chapter 6

The Good Samaritan

Jesus was a brilliant storyteller and He used stories called
parables to help people understand His teachings about God.
This is one of the best-known parables. Jesus asks people
to love and care for others as much as they love and care
for themselves.

Jesus always surprised people by knowing
Jewish religious rules inside out and back
to front. Many religious leaders and holy
men who had spent their whole lives
studying the laws were jealous of Jesus'
knowledge. So they would ask tricky
questions to try to catch Him out.

One day a lawyer came to Jesus and asked, "What must I do to win eternal life?"

"What does the law tell you to do?" Jesus answered simply.

"To love God with all my heart and soul, and to love my neighbour as I love myself," the lawyer reeled off smugly, showing off his knowledge.

"Exactly," said Jesus. "If you already know, why are you asking me?"

"Ah, but who is my neighbour?" the man asked, feeling confident that he had posed a question far too difficult for Jesus to answer.

"Let me tell you a story," Jesus said, without a moment's hesitation. "There was once a man travelling on the road from

Jerusalem to Jericho. Suddenly a group of bandits sprang out from behind some rocks and attacked him. There was no one around to hear the traveller's cries for help. The bandits beat him, robbed him of all his possessions and left him for dead.

"After a while, a priest came walking down the road," Jesus continued. "He wondered what a bundle of rags was doing in the middle of the road and went over to have a look. As soon as the priest saw that the heap was actually a man lying bleeding in the dust, he quickly crossed to the other side of the road. He didn't want to know what had happened or have anything to do with it."

The lawyer gasped, "How could such a

holy man not help someone in need?"

"The next traveller to approach was a Levite," Jesus carried on.

"This man is sure to help," said the Lawyer. Jews from the tribe of Levi were so god-fearing that priests were always chosen from among them.

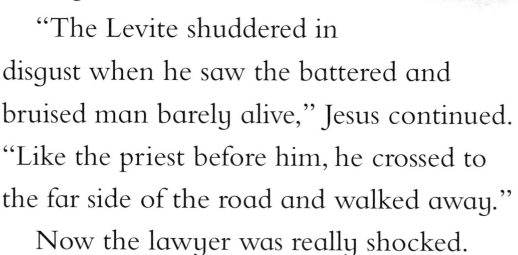

"The Levite shuddered in disgust when he saw the battered and bruised man barely alive," Jesus continued. "Like the priest before him, he crossed to the far side of the road and walked away."

Now the lawyer was really shocked.

A holy Levite should have known better. "Next, a Samaritan passed by," Jesus announced. The lawyer pulled a face. Samaritans were the people who had been sent to live in Israel when the Jews were taken away as slaves by the Babylonians. The Jews hated the Samaritans for taking their land. They also looked down on the Samaritans because they weren't God's Chosen People and often didn't worship God at all. The lawyer thought the Samaritan probably went over to see if there was anything left to steal!

But Jesus continued, "The Samaritan was appalled when he saw the dying man and rushed to help. He gave the poor man some water, heaved him up onto his donkey and hurried to the nearest town. There he paid an innkeeper to take him in and look after him until he was better."

The lawyer was flabbergasted.

"Now which of the three travellers would you say was the neighbour of the attacked man?" Jesus asked.

"The one who helped him," stuttered the lawyer.

"Right," said Jesus. "Now go and behave like the Samaritan."

Luke chapter 10

A Story of Forgiveness

Jesus told this parable about a father and his son who has behaved badly. Sometimes, it can be hard to forgive, but Jesus wanted people to see that God is like the father in the story — He forgives people who are truly sorry.

Jesus told a story about a farmer who had two sons. The farmer was teaching his sons all about farming so that when he passed away, they could take over. However one day, the younger son approached his father with an idea.

"I've been thinking, father," he said

nervously. "I'm grown up and it's time I saw a bit of the world. It would help if I could have my share of the farm now in cash."

The farmer loved his sons dearly and he didn't even have to think about the decision. He counted hundreds of silver coins into bags and handed them to the excited lad.

"Thank you, father," he said, packing his bags to set off. "You won't regret it."

And the farmer watched with tears in his eyes as his younger son left home.

For a while the farmer's son had a wonderful time. He lived like a prince, visiting the finest cities, eating out every night and going to parties. He was surrounded by people who wanted to be his friend, but the problem was they helped him spend all his money. When the silver was gone, his friends vanished too. The young man found himself alone and far from home, without even a few pennies to buy a loaf of bread. To make matters worse, a dreadful drought swept through the land, causing a terrible famine. The farmer's son couldn't even beg for food because no one had enough for themselves. Luckily, he found a job as a pig-keeper. But the wages were pitiful. He had hardly enough money left to buy food after paying his rent. Some days he was so hungry he nearly ate the food for the pigs!

One day, he decided enough was

enough. "I want to go home," he groaned. "I'll beg my father for his forgiveness for being such an idiot. He's bound to be furious, but maybe if I grovel, he'll let me stay and work as one of his farm labourers."

The miserable, ragged young man arrived home and couldn't believe how overjoyed his father was to see him. "I've worried about you and missed you every day, son," the farmer cried, hugging and kissing him.

The ashamed son sobbed as he told his father what had happened.

"Never mind," the farmer said, to his son's utter astonishment. "You're back home now and we're together again. That's all that matters."

Later, the farmer's elder son came home from a hard day's work in the fields to find a party in full swing. The neighbours had been invited over to celebrate his son's return, and a feast had been prepared. There was music, dancing and the people were drinking wine.

"Whatever's going on here?" he gasped, and one of the servants explained what had happened.

The farmer swung his elder son round in

a jig. "Rejoice!" he cried. "Your little brother has finally come back home!"

"What do you mean, 'rejoice'?" the elder son spat, completely furious. "I've stayed with you all these years, working my fingers to the bone, and you've never given me so much as a thank you – let alone thrown me a party! Then HE turns up, having wasted most of your fortune, and you're celebrating how wonderful he is!"

"You have no idea how much your faithfulness means to me," the farmer said to his elder son, drawing him close in a hug. "Everything I have, I give to you. But today is a day to be glad, for your brother was lost and gone forever, but he has come home."

Luke chapter 15

The Pharisee and the Tax Collector

Jesus often used stories to challenge people's ideas and make them think differently. The people listening to Him tell this story would have been surprised to learn that the hero turned out to be the unpopular tax collector, rather than the strictly religious Pharisee.

The Pharisees were Jews who had been brought up to live according to strict religious rules. They believed that their ways of living were the right ways – the only ways – and everyone who didn't follow their rules were not as good as them.

However, Jesus often warned the

Pharisees that they were committing all sorts of sins without realizing it. One was the sin of looking down on others, and He told this story to try to make the Pharisees think about it.

"Two men went into the temple to pray. One was a Pharisee," the Pharisees in the crowd of listeners all smiled smugly, "and one was a tax collector," people booed and hissed at the thought of the traitors who worked for the Romans. "The Pharisee strode straight into the middle of the temple," Jesus continued, "in full view of the people around. He lifted his arms, raised his eyes to the heavens and prayed in a loud, confident voice so that everyone could clearly hear him. 'Thank you, O God,' he said, 'for making me better than common sinners. Thank you for not making me a liar or a cheat like most people. Thank you for giving me the strength to fast twice a week and the generosity to give part of everything I earn to charity. Thank you for not

making me like that greedy tax collector over there.'

"The tax collector was lurking behind a pillar in the shadows, trying his best not to be noticed by anyone. He knelt and bowed his head low, whispering, 'Lord, I am a sinner. I ask for forgiveness, even though I am not worthy of your mercy.'

"Now," finished Jesus, "That day it was the tax collector who went home with God's blessing. For those who set themselves up high will one day fall, and those who think of themselves as lowly will one day be raised up."

Of course the Pharisees didn't like that particular story one little bit.

Luke chapter 18

Jesus and the Children

The crowds that followed Jesus were made up of adults and children alike. Jesus liked having children around Him because they made him smile and laugh. He stopped the disciples when they tried to send the children away. After all, the Kingdom of Heaven belongs to them.

The twelve disciples were travelling with Jesus along a road one day. They began to fall behind, squabbling among themselves. Their argument was about which of them would be the greatest in the Kingdom of Heaven. They thought that Jesus couldn't hear them, but He did. They

were saying things like, "Well, I should be the greatest because I'm Jesus' oldest friend…" And, "I should be the greatest because I've performed the most miracles…" And, "No, I'm sure I'll be the greatest because I pray the most often."

Jesus didn't stop them, He just listened to every word. But later on when they had reached their destination and sat down to rest, He asked, "So what were you all talking about on the road then?"

The disciples felt embarrassed to think that Jesus had heard them trying to outdo each other. No one admitted a thing, but Jesus knew all about what had gone on. "If you really want to be the greatest in God's eyes, you must put others before yourself,"

He told the red-faced men. Jesus reached out to a little girl who was passing by and drew her towards Him. "You must be like this child," He said. "You must have simple, honest values and take genuine delight in helping others. Never look down on children, for they are selfless and giving. They are among the greatest in Heaven."

However, it didn't take long for the disciples to forget what Jesus had told them. A few weeks later, Jesus had been preaching all day long when a group of people with young children approached, asking Him to bless them. Some of the children clung to their parents, while others were playful and pestered Jesus for attention.

Jesus' disciples were sure that this would

be annoying for the weary preacher and they began to shoo the children away. But Jesus stopped his friends. "Let the children come to me," He instructed. "After all, the Kingdom of Heaven belongs to them." Jesus picked up the smallest child and let others scramble onto his lap, blessing them all. "Unless you are pure and wholehearted like these children," He warned his disciples once more, "you will never see God."

Matthew chapters 18, 19;
Mark chapters 9, 10;
Luke chapters 9, 18

Jesus the Good Shepherd

*Jesus told a story to the people around Him
to explain how He saw Himself. Jesus wanted them to
understand that He cared for all people in the way
that a good shepherd looked after his sheep.*

Jesus once said to a crowd that had gathered to hear him speak, "What would a shepherd do if wolves attacked the sheep in his flock? If he was a hired shepherd, doing his job only for the money, he wouldn't stay and fight off the wolves. He would run away and save himself,

leaving the sheep to be eaten. I am not like that shepherd, I am the good shepherd. I will look after my sheep even if it means I have to die for them. I have flocks in other places too, which I need to gather so I can look after all my animals together. My sheep know my voice, they will listen to me and follow me anywhere. It's because I will give up my life for my sheep willingly – for love, not any other reward – that God loves me and will give me my life back again."

Many of Jesus' listeners were bemused by these words. "He must be mad," some of them mumbled. "Do you think it's demons inside Him that are talking?"

But others knew that Jesus was trying to get them to understand something important. "Of course He's not mad!" they insisted, even though they weren't sure what Jesus meant. "How could someone possessed by demons miraculously heal people?"

What Jesus wanted everyone to know was that He genuinely cared for them. Not just for Jewish people, but for people everywhere who wanted to follow God. He was also warning that He was ready to die for everybody, if that is what He had to do. Jesus was explaining that it is only by loving everyone and willingly helping other people in this world, that God will reward us with new life in the next.

John chapter 10

Bartimaeus, the Blind Beggar

*Blind Bartimaeus was an outcast, but he had faith in Jesus
and His healing. When Bartimaeus heard that Jesus was coming
to his town, he made sure that Jesus heard him in the crowd.
He was sure that Jesus could give him back his sight.*

Bartimaeus had been a blind beggar in Jericho for as long as anyone could remember. No one knew how old he was, probably not even Bartimaeus himself, but everyone knew who he was. He could always be found sitting in the same spot by the roadside. His begging bowl set on the ground in front of him, and lifting his poor, dull eyes hopefully to each passer-by.

One day Bartimaeus became aware of quite a fuss building around him. "What's going on?" he asked. "Why are there so many people around?"

"Jesus of Nazareth is coming this way," someone replied.

At once, Bartimaeus' heart began to beat faster. He had heard many stories about the great preacher – how He had given the gift of sight to hundreds of blind people just like him. Jesus had healed paralyzed people, cured the lame, made the sick well again. It was rumoured that Jesus had even brought people back from the dead.

As the crowds bustled around the beggar,

he stumbled to his feet and added his voice to theirs. "Jesus! Have pity on me!" he shouted as loud as he could.

"Be quiet, Bartimaeus! Shut up!" came voices from around him. "Jesus is coming and we want to hear what he is saying."

But that just encouraged old Bartimaeus to shout even louder. "Jesus of Nazareth! Help me!" he bellowed, with a strength he didn't know he had. "I'm over here. Please take pity on me!"

Suddenly, the commotion all around him fell silent and he felt a hand on his shoulder.

"My friend, I'm here," came a soft voice. "How would you like me to help you?"

Trembling, Bartimaeus gasped, "Oh Lord, please let me see."

The ragged man felt gentle fingertips touch his eyelids. Then all at once the darkness before him began to lighten and brighten until he could make out blurs… then shapes and colours… He could see! The world was unimaginably beautiful, and Bartimaeus looked at Jesus' smiling face.

"Your faith has made you well," Jesus said, and Bartimaeus followed Him, dancing in celebration along the road.

Matthew chapter 20; Mark chapter 10; Luke chapter 18

The Parable of the Lost Coins

This parable is about a prince who entrusts his wealth to three of his servants when he goes to another land. Some of the servants use the money sensibly, but one doesn't. Jesus wanted people to use the gifts that God had given them wisely, and not waste them.

Despite everything Jesus had told His followers, there were many people who thought that He was going to establish God's Kingdom by forming an army and marching against the Romans. Jesus knew that He wasn't going to win any earthly revolution. In fact, He was going to be arrested, put on trial and then executed. The Kingdom of Heaven would come at the end of the world, after Judgement Day, and only God knew when that would be. So Jesus told a parable that he hoped would help people make the most of everything God had given them, while they were waiting.

"There was once a prince who had to travel far away to lay claim to a kingdom that was rightfully his," Jesus began. "Before he went, he called his three most trusted servants and asked them to look after his property while he was away. To the first servant he gave five bags of gold. To the second servant he gave two bags and to the third servant he gave one bag. 'Use my money wisely and well,' he bade them.

"The prince left and years passed. Eventually he returned, now a great king. 'What did you do with my gold,' he asked his servants.

"The first servant traded with his five bags of gold and earned five more. The king was delighted and made him governor of ten of his new cities.

"The second servant had saved his two bags of gold in a bank, where it had doubled with interest making four bags. The king was pleased and made him governor of five new cities.

"The last servant had hidden his bag of gold in the ground. 'You mean to say you did nothing with my gift?' the king roared furiously. 'You made no use of it at all?' He turned to his guards. 'Take this man's gold and then throw him out,' he commanded. 'Give the gold to the servant who already has ten bags. For those who try hard will be rewarded, while those who do not will lose what little they have.'

Matthew chapter 25; Luke chapter 19

Jesus Warns of the Future

As Jesus continued preaching to crowds, the religious authorities had been plotting against Him. Jesus begins to prepare His disciples for the suffering and death that is to come because He has foreseen His own death.

There came a rare moment when Jesus found Himself alone with His disciples, walking along a road. He took the opportunity to talk with them. "I sometimes call myself 'the Son of Man'," He began. "What do you think I mean by that?"

"Some people believe you are John the

Baptist," one disciple shrugged.

"Or the prophet Elijah come back from the dead," another suggested.

"Or a new, greater prophet," a third said.

"But who do you think I am?" He asked.

"I think you are the Messiah, the Son of the Living God," Peter announced firmly.

"Then God has blessed you," Jesus said to Peter. "Your name means 'rock', and you are the rock on which I will build my church. I will give you the keys to Heaven, and whatever rules you set on Earth will also stand in Heaven."

Jesus turned to everyone and said gravely, "I must warn you all that things are soon going to get very difficult. The time is drawing near when I must go to

Jerusalem. I will go through much suffering," Jesus gave a sigh. "And eventually I will be put to death." The disciples gasped, but Jesus held up his hands to silence them. "However, three days later, I will come back to life."

The disciples were amazed.

"Are you ready to follow me into hardship and sorrow — even to die for me?" Jesus asked his friends. "If you are, I cannot grant you a reward in this world, but I can promise you joy in the next." Jesus' friends walked on with heavy, but determined, hearts.

Matthew chapter 16; Mark chapter 8; Luke chapter 9

Jesus Shows Himself in Glory

This event is known as the Transfiguration because Jesus was transformed in a blaze of holy light. He is said to have appeared with Moses, the giver of the law, and Elijah, the greatest prophet, and the voice of God was heard saying that Jesus was His son.

One week had passed since Jesus told his disciples that He was the Messiah and warned them of the troubles to come. Now He asked Peter, James and John to go with Him up a hillside a little way to a quiet place where they could pray away from everyone else.

The four men were soon deep in prayer, unaware of anything else around them. But suddenly something made Peter, James and John stop talking to God and turn to look at Jesus. They were shocked to see their kneeling friend so transfixed in prayer. His body looked still and lifeless like a statue, as if His spirit had left it. Jesus' face began to glow brighter and brighter, and His clothes glared whiter and whiter, until He was surrounded by a blaze of glory. It hurt their eyes to look at Him, so they shielded them with their hands. Two other gleaming figures appeared whom they recognized as the great prophets, Moses and Elijah. They listened as Jesus discussed with them what He would have to face in Jerusalem,

including His own death.

Then suddenly a towering black cloud surged overhead. "This is my Son, the Chosen One. Listen to Him!" boomed a mighty voice. The disciples were terrified.

When they looked up again, everything had returned to normal. "Don't tell anyone what you have seen," Jesus commanded, "until I have died and risen from the dead."

Matthew chapter 17; Mark chapter 9; Luke chapter 9

The First Palm Sunday

This story is about the first event in what was to be the last week of Jesus' life. The disciples and friends of Jesus went with Him to Jerusalem to celebrate Passover. Little did they know that dramatic events were about to unfold.

It was the week before the great feast of Passover. Jews from far-off lands travelled to Jerusalem for the celebrations, which lasted several days. Jewish holy men such as the chief priests and Pharisees were waiting to see if Jesus would dare visit the city too. They had been plotting for a long time to arrest and execute the preacher who they thought was stirring up the people and leading them astray. The Jewish leaders thought Jesus might enter Jerusalem unnoticed by mingling among the crowds, so they sent spies through the city to see if they could spot Him.

However Jesus was planning to arrive quite openly. When He and His disciples were a little way off, on the Mount of Olives, Jesus sent two of His friends into the village of Bethphage to find a donkey for him to ride. "You will find one tethered to a doorway," He told them. "Untie it and bring it to me. If anyone objects, just explain that it's me who needs it and they won't stop you."

The disciples found the donkey, just as He had said. When the owners heard who wanted it, they brought it to Jesus themselves. They even threw their cloaks onto the donkey's back to make a comfortable saddle for Him to sit on. The little animal had never been ridden before, but it stood calm and willing as Jesus climbed onto it.

Jesus patted the donkey's head, then set off for the city of Jerusalem. When people along the way saw Him coming, they cheered, sang and danced for joy. The ancient prophets had said that the Messiah would ride into Jerusalem on a donkey. And so the people realized that Jesus was claiming openly for the first time that He

was the saviour they had been waiting for. "Hosanna!" they shouted, lining the donkey's path with their cloaks and palm leaves. "Blessed is He who comes in the name of the Lord! Hosanna in the highest!"

People jammed the streets to welcome Jesus all the way into Jerusalem.

"This is outrageous!" the furious Pharisees bellowed at Jesus. "You're making these people think you're the Messiah!"

"Even if they were quiet," Jesus replied, "the stones would cry out to greet me."

Matthew chapter 21; Mark chapter 11; Luke chapter 19; John chapters 11, 12

Jesus and the Temple Traders

Jesus was angry to see the way the great temple in Jerusalem was being used to make money, even from the poorest people. In fury, Jesus lost His temper and knocked down the traders' stalls to return the temple to a place of worship.

As all good Jews did at the feast of Passover, Jesus went to pray at the great temple. He expected to see the courtyards filled with respectful worshippers deep in prayer, moving quietly about so as not to disturb others. Instead, Jesus was horrified to find the sacred building being used as a market-place.

Everywhere He looked, there were stallholders selling doves and other animals for sacrifices. They cried out their wares, competing for business. People bartered with them, trying to get the best prices, while doves cooed and lambs bleated. Among the stalls were money-changers, haggling with worshippers and counting out foreign money into Jewish shekels. All the traders were charging unfair prices, and the worshippers had no choice but to pay. Everyone had to offer a sacrifice and give shekels to the temple funds at Passover. Meanwhile, city traders were using the temple courtyards and corridors to get from one side of Jerusalem to another.

As Jesus stood amid the hubbub, he grew more and more furious. Suddenly, He began sending the traders' tables flying into the air, kicking down stalls, smashing dove cages open and ripping animal tethers loose. "This is the house of God, but you have turned it into a robbers' den!" He yelled, clearing the temple of everyone except for genuine worshippers.

It wasn't long before the courtyards were full again. This time, with people who had come to hear Jesus preach.

Matthew chapter 21; Luke chapter 19

The Last Supper

This Passover supper was the last meal that Jesus ate with His disciples. Every time Christians celebrate Holy Communion, Mass or the Eucharist, they remember what happened at this meal. Bread is eaten and wine is drank to represent the body and blood of Jesus.

The Jewish leaders were extremely frustrated at their failure to get rid of Jesus. One night they gathered at the house of the chief priest, Caiaphas, for an emergency meeting. They were in the middle of discussing what they could do next when there was a knock at the door.

A servant ushered in a most unexpected guest. It was Judas Iscariot, one of Jesus' twelve disciples and closest friends.

"I'm here because I can give you what you want," he said, his eyes glinting coldly. "Jesus of Nazareth – how much is He worth to you?"

The Jewish officials didn't know what had made Judas become a traitor – and they didn't care either. They could hardly believe their good luck. They put their heads together for a few moments and then announced, "Thirty pieces of silver."

Without a word, Judas held out his hand and Caiaphas counted out the coins. From then on, Judas stayed by Jesus' side, waiting for the opportunity to betray Him.

Mysteriously, Jesus knew everything. With a heavy heart, He prepared for one last meal with his disciples – the Passover supper. He organized a room in secret, so that the Jewish leaders would not find out where He was, and only told His twelve friends about it at the last minute.

The disciples were in a very serious mood as they gathered together. After all, Jesus had warned them two days earlier that He was about to fall into the hands of His enemies and be put to death. As everything Jesus said came true, they were extremely worried.

While they settled at the table, Jesus wrapped a towel around his waist and filled a bowl with water. The disciples were shocked to realize He was going to wash the dust from their feet – a job usually done by the very lowliest servant. Peter was especially shocked and tried to stop Jesus kneeling before him, but Jesus insisted. "I am setting you all an example," Jesus said afterwards. "Always put others before yourself."

Then it was time for dinner. Jesus took a loaf of bread and asked for God's blessing over it. "This is my body," He said with great sadness, "which will be given up for you." He broke the bread and gave it to all the disciples to eat. Then Jesus poured a cup of wine and asked for God's blessing over that too. "This is my blood," He announced gravely, "the sign of a new promise from

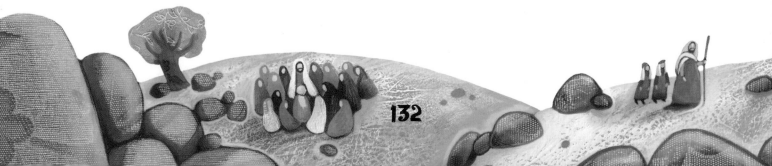

God. My blood will be spilt so that everyone's sins will be forgiven." One by one, the disciples took the cup and drank.

Then Jesus gestured for everyone to begin sharing out the different dishes

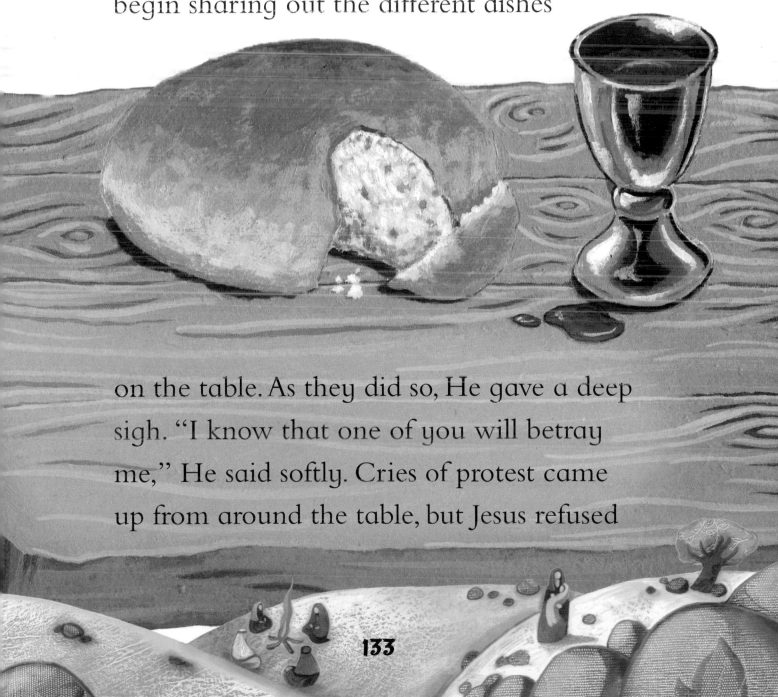

on the table. As they did so, He gave a deep sigh. "I know that one of you will betray me," He said softly. Cries of protest came up from around the table, but Jesus refused to explain further. As the disciples reluctantly turned back to eating, Peter murmured to John, who was sitting closest to Jesus, "Ask Him which of us He means."

John leaned over and spoke in Jesus' ear.

He whispered back, "The one to whom I will give this piece of bread."

John told Peter, and they watched as Jesus tore some bread and offered it to Judas Iscariot. "Do whatever you have to," Jesus told His disloyal friend, "but do it quickly."

And without a word Judas got up from the table and left the room.

Matthew chapter 26; Mark chapter 14; Luke chapter 22; John chapter 13

The Garden of Gethsemane

Full of sadness, Jesus went to the Garden of Gethsemane to pray with His closest friends. When He needed the support of His friends, they were fast asleep. So Jesus prayed to God to give Him strength for the suffering to come. Then the silence of the garden was broken by the sounds of swords and chains.

After Jesus had shared His last supper with the disciples, He sat back and looked around at His dear friends. "I give you a new commandment," He said. "Love each other as I have loved you. By doing this, everyone will know that you are my followers."

"Lord, you've been talking all night as if you're leaving us," Peter protested.

"Yes," Jesus said gently. "I am going away, and where I am going you won't be able to follow me – for a while, at least."

"Why can't I follow you now?" Peter cried out. "I am ready to die for you!"

But Jesus smiled sadly. "Are you really, my friend?" He asked. "By the time this night is out and the cock has crowed three times at dawn, you will have denied three times that you even know me."

"Never," Peter said, choking with sorrow. "Never." And all the disciples agreed strongly.

"Don't be upset," Jesus tried to comfort them. "I am going to prepare a place for you in my Father's house. And I will return to you for a short while, before I have to go away again for good. Even then when you will no longer be able to see me, I will always live in your hearts. Later, when the time is right, you will follow and we will be together again. Until then, do what I have done tonight as a way of remembering me. Be at peace, and be happy for me that I am going to be with my Father."

Jesus looked around at His friends' gloomy faces.

"Now come," He said gently. "Let's go to the Mount of Olives. I would like to pray in the Garden of Gethsemane for a while."

As they walked through the moonlight together, Jesus gave the disciples many more

important instructions. He knew He only had a short time left in which to talk to them. When they finally reached the entrance to the Garden of Gethsemane, Jesus saw that the anxious men were exhausted. "Rest here while I go and pray," He told most of them. But He turned to Peter, James and John and said, "I know you are tired, but would you come with me?"

The three were only too pleased to keep Jesus company. They had never seen Him look so strained and troubled before.

"My heart feels like it's breaking," Jesus sighed heavily when they had gone a little way. "Will you stay while I pray?"

Peter, James and John watched as Jesus

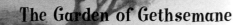

sank to his knees, His head
in His hands.

"Father!" He cried
silently. Jesus prayed that
perhaps He might not have to
face the suffering He knew lay
ahead.

After a long while, Jesus
turned to Peter, James and John
but saw they had fallen asleep.

So Jesus prayed again. He felt the sins of
all the world weighing on His shoulders and
He knew the full horror of what was to
come.

Once more Jesus turned to his friends,
but they were still asleep.

And Jesus prayed again, willingly

accepting the suffering He had to face, so that all people could one day reach God.

At last Jesus finished praying. Peter, James and John were still asleep. But at that moment Judas Iscariot arrived, accompanied by a band of guards. At the noise of guards' swords and chains and the light from their flaming torches, the disciples woke up, startled. "Master," Judas said calmly, greeting Jesus with his usual kiss.

At that pre-arranged sign, the guards grabbed Jesus. After a brief commotion and panic, the disciples fled for their lives into the darkness.

Matthew chapter 26; Mark chapter 14; Luke chapter 22; John chapters 13, 14, 18

Jesus on Trial

Jesus went on trial before the Sanhedrin, the highest Jewish court, but they bribed witnesses to lie. Then He appeared before King Herod and finally Pontius Pilate, the Roman Governor. Although Jesus was not found guilty, Pilate let the people decide His fate. Jesus was sentenced to be crucified.

That night Jesus was marched into the city of Jerusalem, to the great house of the high priest, Caiaphas. Inside Caiaphas' mansion, Jesus was quizzed by Annas, the former high priest. What did He think about ancient holy writings? What miracles did He claim to have worked? Who did He

think He was?

Jesus refused to answer and was marched to a room full of Jewish officials. They had witnesses who they had paid to lie, accusing Jesus of saying and doing things that were against Jewish law. But the witnesses couldn't get their stories straight!

Finally Caiaphas hissed, "I order you to tell us, under solemn oath, whether you think you are the Son of God."

"I am," He said with grace, "and one day you will see the Son of Man seated at the right hand of the Father in Heaven."

"Blasphemy!" roared Caiaphas, a satisfied gleam in his eyes. Blasphemy was the crime of lying against God for which the punishment was death.

In triumph, the Jewish elders had Jesus blindfolded. They slapped and kicked Him, shouting, "Prophesy for us now, Messiah. Guess who hit you!" And in the morning, they had Jesus brought in front of the Roman governor, Pontius Pilate. Only he could approve an execution.

The news spread around the city and an enormous crowd gathered outside.

Pilate asked Jesus many more questions. Are you really a king? Have you been plotting against the Roman government? Have you been planning a rebellion?

Perplexed, Pilate couldn't find that Jesus had done anything wrong. He ordered that Jesus also be questioned by Herod, the ruler of Galilee, who was in Jerusalem at that

time. But Herod couldn't find Jesus guilty of anything either. Even Pilate's wife told him that she had had a dream in which Jesus of Nazareth was innocent of all charges. "Have nothing further to do with Him," she advised her husband.

Pilate made his decision. He went out onto the balcony of his judgement hall and announced to the waiting crowds, "This man has done nothing to deserve death. He shall be whipped and let go." And Jesus was dragged off for His punishment.

Meanwhile the Jewish officials had mingled with the crowds, persuading them that Jesus was guilty of blasphemy. As Pilate turned to go back into his Judgement Hall, people sent up cries of, "Kill him! Kill Jesus of Nazareth!"

But the Roman governor was deeply disturbed, he did not know what for.

Suddenly he had an idea. Pilate remembered that it was Passover and there was a custom for the governor to release one prisoner of the people's choice. In the cells was a murderer called Barabbas. Pilate felt sure that the people would rather have Jesus released than a violent killer.

"Who shall I pardon – Barabbas or Jesus of Nazareth?" Pilate asked the crowd.

He couldn't believe his ears when the shouts came back, "Barabbas!"

Pilate ordered that Jesus be brought in front of him once more. He had been whipped until blood poured down His back. The guards had mocked him as the King of the Jews, too, by pressing a crown of thorns onto His head.

Now the crowd jeered too.

Pilate had had enough. He called for water and a towel, and washed his hands in front of everyone. "I cleanse myself of this man's blood," he announced.

Then Barabbas was released and Jesus was led away to be crucified.

Matthew chapters 26, 27; Mark chapters 14, 15;
Luke chapters 22, 23; John chapters 18, 19

The Crucifixion

*Crucifixion was introduced by the Romans and it was a
slow and painful way to die. As Jesus hung on the cross, there were
earthquakes and a mysterious darkness fell. Mary Magdalene,
Jesus' mother and His closest friends stood at the foot of cross.
They thought that everything was over…*

Jesus had withstood being marched about
in chains, hours of angry questioning, a
beating from the Jewish officials, and being
brutally whipped by Pilate's guards. The
crown of thorns was still pressed into His
head, sending blood trickling down His
pained-filled face.

Two Roman soldiers lifted a huge, solid wooden cross over Jesus' shoulder – so heavy that He nearly collapsed from the weight of it. Then Jesus staggered onwards, through the streets of Jerusalem and towards the hill outside the city where He and two other criminals were to be executed.

Thousands of people lined the way, watching the procession. Jesus willed Himself forwards, heavy step after heavy step. But eventually He crashed into the dust, utterly exhausted. The angry guards dragged a strong man from the crowd called Simon of Cyrene and ordered him to carry the cross instead.

People in the crowd yelled insults and spat on Jesus as He stumbled by. But Jesus caught sight of the sorrowful faces of many friends He had made too. Many of the women were weeping. "Don't cry for me," Jesus said, "but for yourselves, your children and for the destruction that is to come."

Eventually they reached the place for the execution. It was called Golgotha, meaning 'place of the skull'. A soldier made Jesus lie down on the cross, and long nails were hammered into His hands and feet. "Father forgive them, for they don't know what they are doing," Jesus moaned. A notice was fixed above his head which said 'Jesus of Nazareth, King of the Jews' in three languages. "It shouldn't say that," some

Jewish officials objected. "It should say 'This man said he was the King of the Jews'."

But the Roman governor, Pilate, boomed, "I ordered it to be written just like that and that is the way it will stay!"

The Jewish officials mocked as Jesus' cross was hoisted up high. "You said you're the Son of God – so save yourself!"

As the two criminals were raised on crosses either side of Jesus, one sneered, "Yes, save yourself and save us too!"

"How dare you!" the second thief groaned. "We deserve this, but Jesus is innocent. Lord, remember me when you reach your kingdom."

"I promise you," whispered Jesus, "today you will be with me in paradise."

Even though it was midday, darkness suddenly fell over the land. Close by at the foot of the cross, was Jesus' heartbroken mother, and His close friends including John, Mary Magdalene and Salome.

"Mother, take care of John as if he were your own son," Jesus murmered. "John, look after my mother as if she were your own."

Jesus hung in agony on the cross for three long hours. Then He lifted His head and cried aloud, "My God! Why have you abandoned me?" Somebody rushed to lift a stick with a sponge on the end that had been dipped in wine so He could have a drink. Jesus cried out again, "Father, I give up my spirit into your hands. It is finished." And His head drooped.

At that very moment, the earth rumbled and shook, and rocks split open. People said that the great curtain in the temple ripped from top to bottom. Others said they saw graves open and spirits rise from them.

A Roman officer at the foot of the cross looked up and gasped, "This man truly was the Son of God."

Matthew chapter 27; Mark chapter 15; Luke chapter 23; John chapter 19

The First Easter

For the friends and followers of Jesus, and for all Christians, this was, and is, the greatest miracle of all. Jesus rose from the dead. Even though Jesus had told them all that this would happen, they could hardly believe it.

The evening after Jesus had been put to death, a wealthy Jew called Joseph of Arimathea begged Pontius Pilate to allow him to bury Jesus' body. Pilate agreed. So Joseph went with his friend, Nicodemus, back to Golgotha, where women were still weeping at the foot of His cross. Gently,

Joseph and Nicodemus lifted Jesus' poor, bleeding body down. They wrapped Him in a linen shroud with burial spices and, accompanied by the sobbing women, took Him to a nearby cemetery. There the two men laid Jesus in a small, cave-like tomb that Joseph had already paid for, and rolled a heavy stone across the entrance. Full of grief and with nothing else to do, they left.

Meanwhile, some Jewish officials had been to see Pilate. "Jesus of Nazareth said He would rise up again after three days," they told the Roman governor. "Have soldiers guard His tomb so no one can steal the body, then tell everyone that He's miraculously come back to life." Pilate nodded and sent the men away.

Pilate's guards sat outside Jesus' tomb through the night of that first Good Friday – nothing happened. They kept watch all the next day and again nobody came. But as dawn broke on the Sabbath, the third day, the earth suddenly shook so violently that it knocked the soldiers off their feet. A white light blazed out of the sky and shone over the tomb. Through the glare, the terrified soldiers watched the glowing figure of a man roll away the massive stone from the tomb entrance. The soldiers were scared by what they saw and fled for their lives.

Not long afterwards a group of grieving women arrived at the cemetery to pay their respects at the tomb. They included Jesus' friends Mary Magdalene, Mary the mother of James and John, Salome and Joanna. When they saw that the soldiers were gone and the stone had been rolled away, they screamed in horror.

Someone must have stolen Jesus' body! Inside the tomb where Jesus' body should have been, two shining men were sitting. "Why are you looking for the living among the dead?" the men said. "Don't you remember that the Son of Man said He would rise on the third day?"

Mary Magdalene raced to fetch the

disciples Peter and John. When the two men saw the empty tomb they were full of anger. They went off to try to find out who had taken the body. Mary sank down outside the tomb, sobbing. Then suddenly she sensed someone behind her. Mary span around and through her tears she saw a blurry figure whom she thought must be the cemetery gardener. "Why are you weeping?" the man asked.

"If you moved the body," she begged, "please tell me where to."

The man said just one word.

"Mary."

Mary's heart stood still. Suddenly, she recognized the man – it was Jesus!

"Go now," Jesus said softly, as Mary fell

at His feet, gazing up at Him in wonder. "Find the disciples and tell them that I will soon be returning to my Father."

Meanwhile, the other women who had seen the empty tomb were hurrying homewards when all at once, a man appeared out of nowhere on the road in front of them. "Good morning," He said.

The women were amazed and couldn't believe who they were hearing and seeing.

"Don't be afraid," Jesus said. "Go and tell my disciples to travel to Galilee and I will meet them there soon."

Matthew chapters 27, 28; Mark chapter 16; Luke chapters 23, 24; John chapters 19, 20

Jesus and Doubting Thomas

Not everyone could believe that Jesus was alive. The disciple Thomas had not seen Jesus and he wanted proof. He wanted to see and touch the scars of Jesus' wounds on His hands for himself.

Late morning on the third day after Jesus' death, Mary Magdalene burst into the room where the grieving disciples sat together. "I have seen Jesus!" she cried, flushed with excitement, and told them everything that had happened at the tomb. But as much as the disciples wanted to

believe her, they couldn't.

Meanwhile, two of Jesus' disciples were on their way from Jerusalem to the nearby village of Emmaus. As they walked with heavy hearts, a stranger joined them and began talking. To the disciples' astonishment, the stranger didn't seem to have heard anything of the events everyone was talking about – the death of Jesus and the disappearance of His body. However, he seemed to know the ancient holy writings very well and began explaining them.

"Don't you know that the holy men of old said that the Messiah would have to suffer to win glory?"

Later on the disciples shared a meal with the stranger and he blessed some bread, broke it into pieces and gave it to them. It was only then that they realized who he really was. "Jesus!" they gasped in astonishment. And at that moment, He disappeared.

The disciples hurried back to the city and went straight to tell the others – only to find that Jesus had appeared to Peter too!

Everyone began talking at once, full of excitement and asking to hear the stories again and again. No one noticed the newcomer arrive in their midst.

"Peace be with you," said Jesus, as everyone stood back in fear as though He was a ghost. "Don't be frightened," He said, "it's me. Look – here are the wounds on my hands and feet."

But one disciple was missing – Thomas. When his friends told him what had happened he didn't believe it. Eight days later everyone was gathered again to talk and pray. Halfway through the meeting, Jesus appeared once more. "See for yourself, Thomas," He said. "Come and touch my wounds. Have faith – it's true."

Thomas broke down. "My Lord, it's really you," he sobbed.

"Bless you for believing," Jesus said gently. "But even more blessed are those who won't see me and yet will still believe."

Matthew chapter 28; Mark chapter 16; Luke chapter 24; John chapter 20

The Stranger on the Beach

After He died, Jesus' friends had some extraordinary experiences. This story is a reminder of the first time Jesus went fishing with Peter and his friends, and helped them haul in a great catch of fish.

One evening, some of the disciples gathered at the Sea of Galilee. Peter wanted to take a little boat out and go fishing, just as he used to do in the days when he was a fisherman. Soon he and his friends, including James, John, Thomas and Nathaniel, were sailing out into open waters under a starry sky. How free and peaceful it felt – a welcome relief from the terrible events in the city in recent weeks.

All night, the disciples waited for fish to fill their nets, but when dawn came, they were all empty.

Then a voice floated across the waves. "Have you caught anything?"

Peering into the distance, the disciples could see the figure of a man on the shore.

"No, nothing." they yelled back.

"Try dropping your nets to the right side of the boat," came the voice.

The disciples thought it was worth a try. They soon felt their nets become heavy and they could hardly lift them.

Peter, James and John looked at each

other and they remembered a time in the past when exactly the same thing had happened. "It's Jesus!" they exclaimed.

Peter couldn't wait to finish hauling in the catch and sail to shore, so he dived straight into the water and swam to be the first to reach Jesus.

Before long, Peter and the rest of the friends joined Jesus on the shore, and gathered around a little fire on the beach. They sat roasting fish for breakfast, and it was just like old times.

John chapter 21

The Ascension into Heaven

Jesus had told the disciples that one day He would return to be with God, His Father, in Heaven. After Jesus had told them how they must carry on His work on Earth, the disciples watched as a cloud of light surrounded Jesus and He rose up into the sky.

It was finally time for Jesus to leave the world for good. He gathered his disciples together and walked to the Mount of Olives, a short way from Jerusalem.

"Stay in the city for a while," Jesus told His eleven old friends. "You have already all been baptized once — by John the Baptist, with water. But soon you will all be baptized again – this time with the Holy Spirit. God is going to send you powerful gifts and I want you to use them by going out into the world and telling people in every country about me. Baptize all those who believe in me as my followers, in the name of the Father, the Son and the Holy Spirit. Teach them everything that I have taught you." Jesus looked at His friends' worried faces. "Don't forget," He said gently, "I will be with you always, until the end of time."

With that, Jesus rose up into the air, higher and higher, until He disappeared into a blazing cloud of glory.

As the disciples squinted up at the

dazzling light, it glimmered, gleamed and then faded… Jesus was gone but they carried on gazing up at the empty blue sky.

"Men of Galilee, what are you looking at?" came a voice.

The disciples turned to find two men in glowing robes standing next to them.

"Jesus has gone, but one day He will come back to you in the same way."

Full of wonder and sadness, the disciples were comforted and made their way back to Jerusalem. They knew they would not see Jesus again soon, but were sure that one day He would return in glory.

Matthew chapter 28; Mark chapter 16; Luke chapter 24; Acts chapter 1

The Coming of the Holy Spirit

Just as Jesus had promised, the Holy Spirit came to the disciples, now known as the apostles. Flames flickered above their heads and they felt amazing energy. It gave them inspiration and courage to carry on the work that Jesus had begun.

The disciples were in Jerusalem waiting for the Holy Spirit to come and baptize them, as Jesus had told them. Meanwhile they decided to replace the traitor, Judas Iscariot, with a new disciple. Then they would be twelve once more, as Jesus had originally intended. They prayed for guidance, and cast votes and Matthias was chosen. The twelve became known as the apostles. Then the waiting continued.

Fifty days after Passover and the death of Jesus, it was the feast of Pentecost – when Jews celebrated how God had given their religious laws to Moses. The apostles were celebrating the feast, when suddenly a mighty sound like a rushing wind filled their ears as though it was all around them in the house. The apostles felt alive and full of energy, and turning to each other in astonishment, they saw that every man had a tiny flame hovering over his head.

"It must be the Holy Spirit!" they cried, and they found they were all speaking in different languages.

Realizing they had been blessed with the special gifts Jesus has talked about, the apostles excitedly ran out into the streets. Some found themselves giving thanks to God in Greek. Others were preaching about Jesus in Latin. Some were praising the Holy Spirit in Arabic, and many other languages.

Many worshippers from foreign lands had come to Jerusalem for Pentecost and they were stunned. "These men are from Galilee!" they marvelled. "How can they speak our language?"

However, some people just laughed and said that the apostles were drunk.

Then Peter began preaching and everyone who heard him was stirred by his passion. "We are not drunk," he laughed. "We are followers of Jesus of Nazareth. He has risen from the dead, we have seen it with our own eyes. Today we have been blessed by the Holy Spirit with these gifts of languages. Anyone who is truly sorry for their sins and follows the teachings of Jesus will be blessed too. Who wants to join us?"

That day the apostles baptized over three thousand people as followers of Jesus. The foundations of the Christian Church had been laid.

Acts chapters 1, 2

Miracles and Persecution

It was not easy for the apostles to share their message about Jesus, and the authorities began to persecute them too. Peter and John were imprisoned and another apostle, Stephen, was stoned to death. He was the first man to die in the name of Jesus.

Every day after Pentecost, the apostles preached and worked miracles. And each day, more people were baptized as followers of Jesus.

One day, Peter and John were on their way into the temple to pray when they were stopped by a crippled beggar, asking

for a few coins. "We have no money," Peter explained, "but what we do have I will give you… In the name of Jesus, get up and walk!" Peter reached out for the beggar's hand and encouraged him to get to his feet. The ragged man stood up and took a few unsteady paces. Then he began to dance with joy – and he danced all the way into the temple behind Peter and John.

The many worshippers there were utterly amazed. So Peter began speaking aloud, telling everyone about Jesus, how He had risen from the dead and about their God-given gifts of healing. Suddenly, some Jewish officials appeared. They were furious that the name of Jesus was once more causing a commotion among everyone in the temple. They had Peter and John thrown into prison for two days. But the men had committed no crime so they were freed.

Like all of the apostles, Peter did many astounding things in Jesus' name. He seemed to know things that he couldn't possibly know – unless God Himself had told him. He also performed many other great miracles of healing.

Sick people came from all over the country to sit in the streets of Jerusalem just in case Peter passed by. They believed that even if his shadow fell upon them, they would be cured. Of

course, this enraged the Jewish officials further. Jesus was dead, but His name was still stirring up the people so the Jewish officials put Peter and John in prison once more. However that very night they found that the two men had vanished! Upon finding the two apostles teaching in the temple, the Jewish officials' explanation was that an angel had come and released them. The confused, furious officials then had Peter and John beaten, and ordered them never to speak the name of Jesus again.

Of course, this didn't stop the apostles. Every day, the number of followers of Jesus grew. The time came when the Jewish officials finally decided that enough was enough and they accused one apostle,

Stephen, of blasphemy and stoned him to death. He was the first man ever to die in the name of Jesus. Next they sent soldiers to every house in Jerusalem, and then through the rest of Judea too, searching for other followers to arrest. Little did the officials know they were part of God's great plan. The apostles fled to safety to lands far and wide, taking the word of Jesus to many thousands of people who wouldn't otherwise have heard it.

Acts chapters 2, 4, 5, 7, 8

A Narrow Escape

Peter, the leader of the apostles, was a wanted man by King Herod, who despised all Christians. Finally Peter was arrested and imprisoned, but God was with him and helped him escape.

As he travelled around, Peter worked many miracles in the name of Jesus. In a town called Lydda, in north-east Judea, he healed a paralyzed man. In the town of Joppa, he brought Tabitha, a woman who had died, back to life. Only Jesus Himself and the great prophets Elijah and Elisha had ever been granted this gift. Peter preached to Jews and non Jews alike, because he knew that everyone was equal in the eyes of God. He also baptized the first non Jews to follow Jesus.

Meanwhile, King Herod Agrippa became just as determined as the Jewish officials to get rid of the 'trouble-making' Christians. He was a wicked man and he had James, the brother of John, put to death. Then he had Peter the leader of the apostles arrested and put on trial. Flung into a dungeon, Peter was chained to two soldiers, with a round-the-clock guard outside his door. Herod heard how Peter and John had escaped from prison before, and was taking no chances.

But the night before Peter was to be tried, he dreamt that a light blazed into his cell and an angel woke him. "Get up quickly!" the angel commanded. Peter felt his chains fall away, realizing that it wasn't a dream. Then he followed the angel past the guards and out into the street.

The next day, when Herod heard of Peter's escape, he sent soldiers out after him. But Peter was nowhere to be found.

Acts chapters 9, 10, 12

The Road to Damascus

Originally called Saul, Paul was determined to stamp out Christianity, but an extraordinary experience transformed his life. Paul became a Christian missionary, spreading the good teachings of Jesus. The letters that he wrote to the new Christian churches are in the Bible.

One of the Jewish officers who was determined to wipe out Christians was a young man called Saul. He became famous and feared as a ruthless persecutor of the followers of Jesus. Saul had been brought up as a Pharisee – a very strict Jew – and he felt that Jesus' apostles were

undoing all the ancient laws he held to be important. Saul had decided to seek out Christians – not just in Jerusalem, or even Judea, but in other countries too. He went to the high priest in Jerusalem and asked for letters of introduction to the synagogues in Damascus, the capital of Syria, so he could find and arrest followers of Jesus there.

Soon Saul was on his way. As the great city loomed before him, a flash of lightning blazed from the sky and struck him off his horse. Saul grovelled in the dirt, shaken to the core. Somehow he knew it hadn't been an accident.

"Saul, Saul, why are you persecuting me?" a voice boomed into his mind.

"Who – who are you?" the terrified Saul

managed to stutter, shutting his eyes against the dazzle.

"I am Jesus, whom you have sworn to persecute," the voice roared. "Now get up, go into the city and wait there."

The voice was gone, the light faded and Saul opened his eyes.

Everything was black… He was blind!

The soldiers accompanying Saul were puzzled. They led him into the city and found a place for him to stay. There Saul sat for two days, refusing to talk to anyone or even eat or drink.

On the third day, there was a knock at the door. Saul's soldiers opened it to an old

man named Ananias. "God has sent me to you," Ananias explained. "He told me that He has chosen you to spread His message – not just to the Jews, but to non Jews too."

Gently, Ananias laid his hands on Saul's head and the darkness gradually became light, as if scales fell from his eyes, and he could see again.

Overwhelmed with relief and joy, Saul fell to his knees and gave thanks to God. Then he asked Ananias to baptize him!

When Saul had recovered from his ordeal, he went straight to the synagogues of Damascus, as he had planned. But instead of arresting Christians, he preached that Jesus was the Son of God.

Acts chapters 8, 9

Paul and Silas in Prison

After becoming a Christian, Paul quickly became a target for persecution and he and his companions were often arrested and imprisoned as they travelled around. In this story, even though they were in prison, Paul and Silas were still able to spread the teachings of Jesus.

At first, people found it difficult to believe that Saul had gone from being a sworn enemy of Jesus to one of his most passionate followers. To give people an outward sign of his change of heart, Saul changed his name to Paul. He managed to win trust by putting even more energy and

effort into finding new followers for Jesus. As a Pharisee, Paul had great knowledge of the ancient sacred writings, and could argue in support of Jesus with the Jewish officials in Jerusalem too. How they came to hate their former favourite, Saul! Eventually the apostles discovered that the officials were plotting to kill Paul, so they sent him far to the north to the city of Tarsus, where he could preach out of danger.

That was the beginning of many years of travelling for Paul, teaching the messages of Jesus to people all around the Mediterranean. Often accompanied by other apostles, such as Barnabas and John, he made one journey after another. He taught non Jews about God, from Syria to

Cyprus, and Turkey to Greece, and baptized thousands in the name of Jesus. However Paul and his friends faced many dangers. Angry Jews hated them for baptizing non Jews, and non Jews hated them for saying that the idols they worshipped were false. Even when Paul and his companions were chased out of town, or suffered violence, they weren't put off. In fact they became even more determined. Every single soul they won for God gave them great joy.

Paul and his fellow apostle Silas were once in Macedonia when they were accused of 'disturbing the peace', and were whipped and thrown into prison. However they refused to be downhearted. They began singing hymns to God, and the other prisoners joined in too.

At midnight, the sudden sound of
rumbling drowned out the apostles' voices.

The prison walls shook and started to
crumble. The terrified prisoners were thrown
from side to side. Their chains broke and
their cell doors burst open.

All the prisoners could have seized the opportunity to escape, but Paul and Silas talked everyone into staying put. When the jailer ran in with his guards, he couldn't believe it. He had been ready to take his own life if all of the prisoners had run away while under his responsibility. The jailer ordered for them to be chained up again, all except for Paul and Silas who were taken to his house. There, the jailer fell on his knees before them and asked them to tell him more about Jesus.

By the time dawn came, the jailer and his whole household had been baptized.

Acts chapters 10, 11, 13 to 16

John's Vision of Heaven

The Bible begins and ends with God. In the first story in the book of Genesis, God created Heaven and Earth. In the last story in the book of Revelation, John sees a vision of a new Heaven and a new Earth in which good has triumphed over evil.

The apostle John was praying one day, when he heard a voice. John span around to see Jesus, shining with light. Jesus said, "I am the first and the last. I am the Living One who was dead. Now I shall live forever. Watch — I will show you the future."

John saw a door opening into Heaven,

revealing God surrounded by singing angels.

He was shown the battle between good and evil playing out on the Earth, and the end of the world when Jesus was triumphant over the devil. God was passing judgement on all people. If a person's name was not in the Lord's great book, they were destroyed.

Then John was shown a new Heaven and Earth, and a vision of a new Jerusalem. Through the city flowed the River of Life. God's Kingdom on Earth had come.

Jesus spoke one last time. "I will be coming soon, and I shall reward the good with blessings forever."

And John whispered, "Amen!"

Revelation chapters 1, 4, 5, 19 to 22

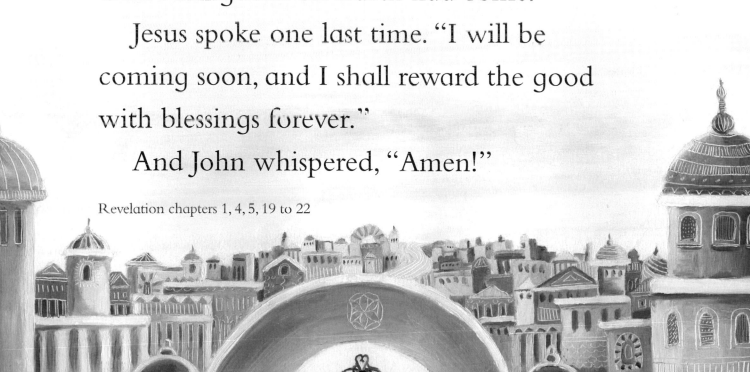

People in the New Testament

Andrew Fisherman and brother of Peter, who became one of Jesus' twelve apostles.

Bartholomew One of Jesus' twelve apostles.

Herod the Great King of Judea at the time Jesus was born. He tried to have Jesus killed.

James Brother of John and son of Zebedee, he became one of Jesus' twelve apostles.

James One of Jesus' twelve apostles.

John One of Jesus' twelve apostles. He was granted a vision of the Kingdom of Heaven.

John the Baptist A prophet who baptized Jesus in the River Jordan.

Joseph Husband of Mary and foster father of Jesus, he was a carpenter who lived in Nazareth.

Judas Iscariot One of Jesus' twelve apostles. He betrayed Jesus to His enemies.

Mary Mother of Jesus and wife of Joseph of Nazareth.

Mary Magdalene A good friend of Jesus. She was the first person to see Him after He had risen from the dead.

Matthew A tax collector who became one of Jesus' twelve apostles.

Peter A fisherman and brother of Andrew, he became one of Jesus' twelve apostles.

Philip Formerly a follower of John the Baptist, he became one of Jesus' twelve apostles.

Simon the Zealot One of Jesus' twelve apostles.

Thaddeus One of Jesus' twelve apostles.

Thomas One of Jesus' twelve apostles. He didn't believe that Jesus had risen from the dead until he had seen Jesus for himself.